ANCIENT GREECE

ANCIENT CIVILIZATIONS IN REVIEW

By Seth Lynch

Enslow Publishing

Please visit our website, www.enslow.com. For a free color catalog of all our high-quality books, call toll free 1-800-398-2504 or fax 1-877-980-4454.

Library of Congress Cataloging-in-Publication Data
Names: Lynch, Seth, author.
Title: Ancient Greece / Seth Lynch.
Description: Buffalo, New York : Enslow Publishing, [2025] | Series: Ancient civilizations in review | Includes index.
Identifiers: LCCN 2024022639 | ISBN 9781978542761 (library binding) | ISBN 9781978542754 (paperback) | ISBN 9781978542778 (ebook)
Subjects: LCSH: Greece–Civilization–To 146 B.C.–Juvenile literature.
Classification: LCC DF77 .L94 2025 | DDC 938–dc23/eng/20211023
LC record available at https://lccn.loc.gov/2024022639

Published in 2025 by
Enslow Publishing
2544 Clinton Street
Buffalo, NY 14224

Portions of this work were originally authored by Daniel R. Faust and published as *Ancient Greece*. All new material this edition authored by Seth Lynch.

Designer: Leslie Taylor
Editor: Kristen Nelson

Photo credits: Cover (parthenon) tilialucida/Shutterstock, (discus thrower) Gilmanshin/Shutterstock.com, (back cover vase) Kamira/Shutterstock.com; Cover and series art (vintage map) Andrey_Kuzmin/Shutterstock.com (brush strokes) ozzichka/Shutterstock.com, (font) MagicPics/Shutterstock.com; p. 5 Sidhe/Shutterstock.com; p. 7 Wolfgang Sauber/ File:AMI - Oktopusvase.jpg_commons.wikimedia.org; p. 9 Georgy Markov/Shutterstock.com; p. 11 Philipp Foltz (1805–1877)/File:Discurso funebre pericles.PNG_commons.wikimedia.org; p. 12 Viacheslav Lopatin/Shutterstock.com; p. 13 (top) mountainpix/Shutterstock.com, (bottom) tilialucida/Shutterstock.com; p. 15 Fletcher Fund, 1926/metmuseum.org; p. 16 See U in History/Shutterstock.com; p. 17 Fletcher Fund, 1956/metmuseum.org; p. 19 Français : Coupe attribuée au Peintre de Triptolème./File:Greek-Persian duel.jpg_commons.wikimedia.org; p. 21 Rogers Fund, 1911/metmuseum.org; p. 23 john antoni/File:Spartan helmet 2 British Museum.jpg_commons.wikimedia.org; p. 25 John Steeple Davis (1844-1917)/File:Destruction of the Athenian army at Syracuse.jpg_commons.wikimedia.org; p. 27 (statue) Gokhan Dogan/Shutterstock.com, (coin) Viacheslav Lopatin/Shutterstock.com; p. 29 canbedone/Shutterstock.com, (inset map) svekloid/Shutterstock.com; p. 30 Marti Bug Catcher/Shutterstock.com.

Printed in the United States of America

CPSIA compliance information: Batch #CWENS25: For further information, contact Enslow Publishing at 1-800-398-2504.

CONTENTS

Words in the glossary appear in **bold** the first time they are used in the text.

By the Sea

One of the oldest European **civilizations** began near the Mediterranean and Aegean Seas where Greece is today. But what is now called **ancient** Greece wasn't just one country. It had many **city-states.** Art and ideas born in ancient Greece spread to countries around the world!

Learn More

Ancient people from the area of present-day Greece called their land Hellas. They called themselves Hellenes.

Ancient Greece
Aegean Sea
Troy
Persian Empire
Athens
Sparta
Mediterranean Sea
Knossos

Beginning on Crete

The Minoans on the island of Crete built the first powerful civilization of ancient Greece. They had a strong navy. Around 1500 BCE, the Mycenaean civilization rose on the Greek **mainland**. The Mycenaeans conquered, or took over, the Minoans around 1400 BCE.

LEARN MORE

The Mycenaean language is the oldest known form of the Greek language.

Minoan vase

Stories say the Mycenaean civilization fought a war with the city of Troy. Shortly after, the Mycenaean civilization fell around 1100 BCE. From then until about 800 BCE, Greece entered a time sometimes called the Dark Age. Historians haven't been able to find writing or art from this time!

LEARN MORE

The Trojan War is part of the well-known stories of *The Iliad* and *The Odyssey*. Homer, an important Greek writer, wrote these stories.

Homer

The Rise of City-States

By about 800 BCE, city-states began to rise. They were independent, which means each had its own government. By the 500s BCE, **democracy** began to form in the city-state of Athens. All the male **citizens** were allowed to take part in running the government.

Learn More

Women, **enslaved** people, and people born in other countries weren't considered citizens in ancient Greece.

Athens became a large and important city-state, known for art and beautiful buildings. Several great thinkers and **poets** lived and worked in Athens. The Parthenon, one of the greatest **temples** in Greece, was built on a hill looking over the city.

LEARN MORE

Athens had control of much of eastern Greece by the 400s BCE, as well as islands in the Aegean Sea and beyond.

the Parthenon

Gods and Goddesses

The people of Greece believed in many gods and goddesses. These gods were a way for the ancient Greeks to understand the natural world. The Greeks went to temples to worship, or honor, their many gods.

LEARN MORE

The most important Greek gods lived on Mount Olympus and were led by Zeus, king of the Greek gods.

The first Olympic Games honored Zeus. People from city-states across the Greek world took part in the Olympics. The Olympics likely began around 776 BCE and were held every four years.

LEARN MORE

The ancient Olympics had wrestling, jumping, and foot races, among other contests.

Persian Invasion

City-states came together in 490 BCE to fight the Persian Empire. Athenian forces played a big part in **defending** Greece. When the Persians came back in 480 BCE, Athens had built up a navy that helped the Greeks win again. Athens grew in strength afterward.

LEARN MORE

An empire is made up of many countries or lands that are led by one government or a single ruler.

Greek and Persian fighters

Ancient Art

The time of ancient Greece called the classical period began around 480 BCE. During this time, Sophocles and Euripides wrote great plays. The **philosopher** Socrates taught during this time too. The arts of the classical period are still studied today!

LEARN MORE

Many later artists, such as Michelangelo, copied the look of ancient Greek art.

21

Strong Sparta

The arts of ancient Greece were centered in Athens. But the city-state of Sparta cared about having a strong army. Its citizens were taught to value bravery and following orders—not art. By 431 BCE, Sparta believed Athens had become too powerful.

LEARN MORE

At age 20, all men who were citizens in Sparta became soldiers, or fighters.

Spartan helmet

To War

Athens and Sparta went to war. They fought for almost 30 years. Though Sparta had a well-trained army, Athens had a wall around the city and a strong navy. Still, in 404 BCE Sparta won. It became the most powerful city-state in ancient Greece.

LEARN MORE

The war between Athens and Sparta is now called the Peloponnesian War.

Part of the Empire

In 338 BCE, King Philip II of Macedon conquered Greece. He united, or brought together, almost all of the Greek city-states. His son, Alexander the Great, became king next. By his death in 323 BCE, Alexander had grown his empire to include Egypt, Persia, and India.

LEARN MORE

Alexander the Great's empire helped spread the Greek culture far and wide. Culture is the beliefs and ways of life of a group of people.

ancient Greek coin showing Alexander the Great

Alexander the Great

Roman Conquerors

Alexander's large empire broke apart over the next almost 300 years. Then, in 30 BCE, the Roman Empire conquered the lands of ancient Greece. The Romans borrowed much of their culture, such as art and some ways of thinking, from ancient Greece.

LEARN MORE

At its largest, the Roman Empire controlled land from present-day England and Spain to North Africa and the Middle East!

the Roman Empire

Timeline of Ancient Greece

c. 3000 BCE....................... The Minoan civilization rises on the island of Crete.

c. 1500–1100 BCE......................... The Mycenaeans control mainland Greece.

c. 1200–c. 800 BCE..... Greece enters the Dark Age.

776 BCE...................... The first Olympics are held.

c. 500 BCE................Athens starts to grow into an important city-state.

490–479 BCE .... The city-states fight the Persian Empire.

431—404 BCE ....Athens and Sparta fight the Peloponnesian War.

338 BCE..... Philip II of Macedon conquers Greece.

30 BCE........ The Roman Empire conquers Greece.

GLOSSARY

ancient: Very old or having to do with times long ago.

citizen: Someone who lives in a country legally and has certain rights.

city-state: A city and the nearby farms and villages under its control.

civilization: Organized society with written records and laws.

defend: To guard against harm.

democracy: The free and equal right of every person to take part in a government.

enslaved: Having to do with being forced to work without pay and against a person's will.

mainland: The main part of a landmass.

philosopher: One who studies philosophy, which is a way of thinking that tries to understand the nature of that which is real.

poet: A person who writes poetry, or pieces of writing in verse that sometimes tell a story.

temple: A building for worship.

FOR MORE INFORMATION

BOOKS

Faust, Daniel R. *The Rise and Fall of Ancient Greece.* Minneapolis, MN: Bearport Publishing Company, 2025.

Redshaw, Hermione. *A Kid's Life in Ancient Greece.* Minneapolis, MN: Bearport Publishing Company, 2024.

WEBSITE

National Geographic Kids: 10 Facts About Ancient Greece

www.natgeokids.com/uk/discover/history/greece/10-facts-about-the-ancient-greeks/

Learn more fun facts about ancient Greece here.

Publisher's note to educators and parents: Our editors have carefully reviewed this website to ensure it is suitable for students. Many websites change frequently, however, and we cannot guarantee that a site's future contents will continue to meet our high standards of quality and educational value. Be advised that students should be closely supervised whenever they access the internet.

INDEX